W9-ASZ-308

To Max and Gus and the students
of the Naval Academy Primary School

—E.R.B.

For my sister, Patti

—K.H.

Copyright © 2006
Printed in China

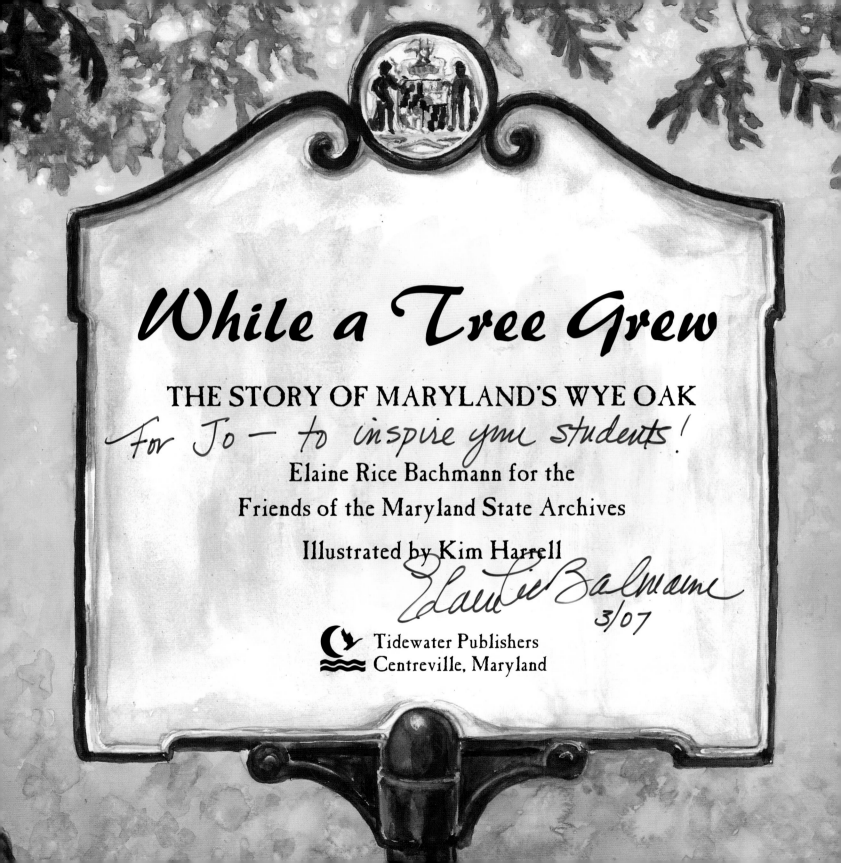

While a Tree Grew

THE STORY OF MARYLAND'S WYE OAK

For Jo — to inspire your students!

Elaine Rice Bachmann for the
Friends of the Maryland State Archives

Illustrated by Kim Harrell

Elaine Rice Bachmann
3/07

Tidewater Publishers
Centreville, Maryland

No ceremony marked the planting of the great Wye Oak
on Maryland's Eastern Shore. Perhaps a squirrel buried
an acorn there, or a bird dropped one nearby. Maybe
someone tossed an acorn over their shoulder
as they walked along.

However it happened, long, long ago, a
sapling took root and a tree began to grow.

And the tree grew while some of the first Marylanders, Indians called the Ozinies and the Wiccomisses, walked and hunted along the ancient Choptank Trail that passed by the tree as it ran along the eastern side of the Chesapeake Bay.

And the tree grew while the Englishman Captain John Smith and his crew explored the rivers and streams of the Chesapeake Bay and told the rest of the world about the beauty and abundance of what they had seen.

They
were soon
followed by
two ships called the
Ark and the *Dove* carrying settlers
from England who founded the colony of Maryland.

And the tree grew while the battles of the Revolutionary War were fought. The grist mill next to the tree produced flour to feed George Washington's army.

And the tree grew along with the town of Wye Mills
whose visitors tied their horses to its limbs, and
the horses' hooves kicked against its roots
creating scars that became the tree's
great knobby knees.

And the tree grew while a little boy named Frederick Douglass worked as a slave on a nearby farm, and then made his way north to devote his life to helping others become free.

And the tree grew while the ancient Indian path became a road and people began to come by automobile to visit the old oak tree.

And the tree grew so big and mighty that it became famous as the largest white oak in North America. People from all over the country came to gaze up into its branches in awe of all the history it had seen.

And the tree grew while the first airplanes flew overhead and while workers, armed with concrete and steel, inched their way across the Chesapeake to build the Bay Bridge.

And the tree grew old. One night, when
the wind blew especially hard, it fell.

And when the tree's limbs and branches were gathered, they were made into treasured reminders of Maryland's great Wye Oak, to be used and admired by people for years to come.

And a part of the tree still
grows in the many seedlings
from its acorns that have taken
root throughout the land.
Maybe one of these, too, will
grow for over 400 years and
become famous.

   However it happened, long,
long ago, a sapling took root
and a tree began to grow.